SHARING THE
Word

SCRIPTURAL REFLECTIONS FOR ADVENT

ARCHBISHOP DANIEL E. PILARCZYK

Franciscan
MEDIA
Cincinnati, Ohio

Excerpts from…
Scripture passages have been taken from *New Revised Standard Version Bible,* copyright ©1989 by the Division of Christian Education of the National Council of the Churches of Christ in the U.S.A., and used by permission. All rights reserved.

Cover and book design by Mark Sullivan
Cover image © Mike Bentley | istockphoto.com

Library of Congress Cataloging–in–Publication Data
Pilarczyk, Daniel E.
Sharing the Word : Scriptural reflections for Advent / Daniel E. Pilarczyk.
   p. cm.
   ISBN 978-1-61636-469-4 (alk. paper)
 1. Advent—Prayers and devotions. 2. Catholic Church—Prayers and devotions. 3. Catholic Church. Lectionary for Mass (U.S.) I. Title.
   BX2170.A4P55 2012
   242'.332—dc23
                        2012011465

ISBN 978-1-61636-469-4

Copyright ©2012, Daniel E. Pilarczyk. All rights reserved.

Published by Franciscan Media
28 W. Liberty St.
Cincinnati, OH 45202
www.FranciscanMedia.org

Printed in the United States of America.
Printed on acid–free paper.
12 13 14 15 16   5 4 3 2 1

INTRODUCTION

The season of Advent is the time when we prepare our hearts to celebrate the birth of Jesus at Christmas. It is a sacred time, the start of the Church's liturgical year, but also a period set aside for reflection, prayer, and good works. It is a season of hope and joyful expectation.

This little book will help you focus on your spiritual journey this Advent. Use it each day for just a few minutes, or longer if you can. In doing so, I'm sure that your spirit will be refreshed, and your preparations for Christmas will go a little more smoothly.

As we share the word this Advent, let us keep the eternal Word, Jesus Christ, foremost in our minds and in our hearts.

First Sunday of Advent

Year A: *Isaiah 2:1–5; Psalm 122:1–2, 3–4, 4–5, 6–7, 8–9; Romans 13:11–14; Matthew 24:37–44*

Year B: *Isaiah 63:16b–17, 19b, 64:2–7; Psalm 80:2–3, 15–16, 18–19; 1 Corinthians 1:3–9; Mark 13:33–37*

Year C: *Jeremiah 33:14–16; Psalm 25:4–5, 8–9, 10, 14; 1 Thessalonians 3:12—4:2; Luke 21:25–28, 34–36*

Besides this, you know what time it is, how it is now the moment for you to wake from sleep. For salvation is nearer to us now than when we became believers; the night is far gone, the day is near.

(Romans 13:11–12)

In his Letter to the Romans, Paul tells us that it's time to wake up. It may seem that we are in a time of darkness, but full daylight is almost here. The universal fulfillment of salvation is nearly upon us.

Paul describes what this awakening involves—getting rid of the attitudes and practices that constitute moral darkness: overindulgence in food and drink, sexual misbehavior, and contentiousness that undermines our relationships. All these have to be taken off like dirty clothes.

As this new Church year begins, God's word says to us, "Get up! Get dressed! Get busy! It's almost light and you've got an important day ahead of you!"

Prayer

Lord, wake me up. Wake up my heart to love you as when I first discovered your love. Wake up my mind to embrace the mystery of your incarnation. Finally, Lord, wake up my weary spirit that I may leap with excitement into these days of preparation. Amen.

Response

What areas of your life need to "wake up" as you prepare for Christmas? Spend some time listening to God today and examine those areas in your life.

Monday of the First Week of Advent

*Isaiah 2:1–5; Psalm 122:1–2, 3–4b,
4cd–5, 6–7, 8–9; Matthew 8:5–11*

In days to come
  the mountain of the Lord's house
shall be established as the highest of the
    mountains,
  and shall be raised above the hills;
all the nations shall stream to it.

(Isaiah 2:2)

We enter the season of Advent with readings from Isaiah, the most prolific of the prophets of the Old Testament, the great proclaimer of the coming of the salvation of the Lord.

God's plans are to come to set things right, to bring all creation to fulfillment. God intends to purify and sanctify his people. He wants to bring them into the final glory of his heavenly city.

If we are to collaborate with God's will, we have to pay attention to his plans. He intends that his glory be shelter and protection for us all, shade from the heat of day, refuge and cover from storm and rain. That's what God wants. That's what we look forward to as we begin another Church year.

Prayer

Come, Emmanuel, into my heart and mind. Reveal to me the way to peace. In this hurried season, stop me in my tracks and teach me your ways. Amen.

Response

Create a plan for this Advent. Each day go through your spiritual plan. Perhaps it is a daily walk with God or journaling time or daily Mass. You and God decide.

Tuesday of the First Week of Advent

*Isaiah 11:1–10; Psalm 72:1, 7–8,
12–13, 17; Luke 10:21–24*

Give the king your justice, O God,
 and your righteousness to a king's son.
May he judge your people with righteousness,
 and your poor with justice.

(Psalm 72:1–2)

This psalm seems to have been an acclamation in honor of a Davidic king.

But the full meaning of the psalm is to be found only in Christ. The earthly king is a figure of Christ the King. This prayer–song looks forward to the king's just rule, his glorious reign, his universal dominion, his defense of the poor and the oppressed, the prosperity of his kingdom. The psalm points to Jesus and to the ultimate fulfillment of his reign.

The season of Advent is about the future, about the coming of the heavenly kingdom, about the gifts being offered to the people by the heavenly king, about the completion of all our hopes.

"Justice shall flourish in his time and the fullness of peace forever."

Prayer

Giver of all good things, teach me to give as you do, abundantly and without price. May my gift-giving come from the heart and reflect your holy name. Amen

Response

What gifts would this heavenly king give to the people on your gift list? Make a new list and include God's suggestions.

Wednesday of the First Week of Advent

Isaiah 25:6–10a; Psalm 23:1–3a, 3b–4, 5, 6; Matthew 15:29–37

Jesus called his disciples to him and said, "I have compassion for the crowd, because they have been with me now for three days and have nothing to eat; and I do not want to send them away hungry, for they might faint on the way."

(Matthew 15:32)

During these first days of Advent, the Church's liturgy gives us readings about the generosity of God, about God's care for his people.

Today in the reading from Matthew 15 we see Jesus healing the sick and feeding the hungry. All kinds of afflicted people are cared for: the deformed, the lame, the blind. Thousands are fed in a single sitting.

The Lord is not tight-fisted with his gifts. There are no limitations on who gets cured, no restrictions on how much food will be provided.

The Lord is still generous to his people, to us. It might be good for us today to reflect on the ways in which we experience the Lord's generosity and to offer him our thanks.

Prayer

Good and gracious God, thank you for winter's beauty and the silence of this holy season. Thank you for the love that surrounds me in my family and friends. But most of all, thank you for your gentle presence in every moment of my day. Amen.

Response

Do something extraordinarily generous in God's name.

Thursday of the First Week of Advent

Isaiah 26:1–6; Psalm 118:1, 8–9, 19–21, 25–27a; Matthew 7:21, 24–27

Trust in the LORD forever,
 for in the LORD GOD
 you have an everlasting rock.
For he has brought low
 the inhabitants of the height;
 the lofty city he lays low.

(Isaiah 26:4–5)

Isaiah continues to instruct God's people about God's providential plans for their future, and what kind of future they can expect.

Today we learn that the future of God's people includes security. When the day of the Lord arrives, the people will sing a song of victory over their enemies. God's city will be impregnable. God will serve as a wall of safety for those who are his own.

This reading invites the people to trust in the strength of God's city and in God's intent to keep it in peace. "Trust in the LORD forever," the prophet says, "for the Lord is an everlasting rock."

God invited trust from his people then. He still does yet today. He is still our rock of safety.

Prayer

O God, I trust in your goodness and mercy. You have been with us from all time, and are the rock on which we stand firm. Bless our efforts to be light for the world, especially now as we wait for the coming celebration of the birth of your son, Jesus. Amen.

Response

Clean out a dark area of your life today. Trust in God to help you in the process.

Friday of the First Week of Advent

*Isaiah 29:17–24; Psalm 27:1, 4, 13–14;
Matthew 9:27–31*

I believe that I shall see the goodness of the
    Lord
  in the land of the living.
Wait for the Lord;
  be strong, and let your heart take courage;
  wait for the Lord!

(Psalm 27:13–14)

This is a prayer of confidence in the Lord's care for me, a plea to be with the Lord.

As we wait for the coming of the Lord during this season of Advent, we turn to the Lord for light, for refuge from whatever would harm us. We long for the Lord's company in his temple together with all who live in him.

Waiting for the Lord calls for courage and determination on our part. There is nothing that we need to be afraid of, nothing that can do us real harm, but at the same time reaching out to the presence of the Lord is not effortless. It requires ongoing effort, and a profound conviction that the Lord is my light and my salvation.

Prayer

Lord, I wait for you. In the deep of this winter season come to me. Assure me that your strength is my own: Your courage inspires me to be unafraid. Your light will warm and lead me on. Amen.

Response

Ask yourself, "Of what am I afraid?" Turn your fear over to God.

Saturday of the First Week of Advent

Isaiah 30:19–21, 23–26; Psalm 147:1–2, 3–4, 5–6; Matthew 9:35—10:1, 6–8

Then he said to his disciples, "The harvest is plentiful, but the laborers are few; therefore ask the Lord of the harvest to send out laborers into his harvest."

(Matthew 9:37–38)

Today's Gospel is from Matthew 9 and 10. Jesus expresses concern for the people he was preaching to. They seemed so needy, so abandoned, so leaderless, like sheep without a shepherd.

Out of compassion for the crowds, Jesus authorizes his disciples to assist in his mission to cure the sick and drive out demons. The disciples were to assure their hearers that God would soon come in glory to establish his kingdom.

Many people in our world are like sheep without a shepherd, wandering aimlessly, seeking a salvation they don't even understand. We are called to bring them into Jesus's flock and help make them ready for his kingdom. In one way or another we are all shepherds of God's flock.

Prayer

Shepherd me, O Lord, beyond my discontent and my disillusionment, beyond my worldly ways, though the darkness and into your marvelous light. Amen.

Response

If you have a sheep in your crèche set, get it out early as a reminder that the Divine Shepherd is caring for you this Advent.

Second Sunday of Advent

Year A: *Isaiah 11:1–10; Psalm 72:1–2, 7–8, 12–13, 17; Romans 15:4–9; Matthew 2:1–12*

Year B: *Isaiah 40:1–5, 9–11; Psalm 85:9–10, 11–12, 13–14; 2 Peter 3:8–14; Mark 1:1–8*

Year C: *Baruch 5:1–9; Psalm 126:1–2, 2–3, 4–5, 6; Philippians 1:4–6, 8–11; Luke 3:1–6*

What sort of persons ought you to be in leading lives of holiness and godliness, waiting for and hastening the coming of the day of God, because of which the heavens will be set ablaze and dissolved, and the elements will melt with fire?

(2 Peter 3:11–12)

When the author of Second Peter calls us to conduct ourselves "in holiness and devotion," he is calling us to be aware of who and what we really are and to behave accordingly. He's calling us to be alert to Christ's life in us and to carry out with consistency the implications of that life in the circumstances of our own particular situation.

This requires some attentiveness and some determination, to be sure, because we are so easily distracted from the really important things in our lives. But it doesn't require extraordinary efforts to make ourselves holy: God has already taken care of that.

This reading seems to suggest that our holiness and devotion will make the world a little more ready for its final righteousness.

Prayer

Heavenly Father, we are all your children. There is no division in your kingdom; we are all loved. Give me a special grace to reach out to those I cannot forgive. Help me to make peace. Amen.

Response

Spend some time today thinking about the ways in which you are already holy, and how that helps bring the message of Jesus Christ into the world.

Monday of the Second Week of Advent

Isaiah 35:1–10; Psalm 85:9ab–10, 11–12, 13–14; Luke 5:17–26

Strengthen the weak hands,
   and make firm the feeble knees.
Say to those who are of a fearful heart,
   "Be strong, do not fear!
Here is your God.
   He will come with vengeance,
with terrible recompense.
   He will come and save you."

(Isaiah 35:3–4)

Isaiah continues his message about the coming of the Lord, a message that is pertinent to us today, among whom there are so many whose faith is feeble.

God is always watering the desert and making highways for his people whether it is a matter of freeing his people from slavery in Egypt or bringing them home from Babylon, whether it is to prepare for the coming of God's Son as man or for the final coming of the Messiah in glory. God is always busy bringing us into freedom.

The Lord may not come immediately and make everything right this very day, but he has promised to come and he will come. God's careful providence for us calls for our attention and our gratitude.

Prayer

Lord, the ride to your kingdom has been a little bumpy lately. Smooth out those rough spots and remind me to stop along the road to notice how good my life really is. Amen.

Response

At the end of this day, thank God for three things you received from him.

Tuesday of the Second Week of Advent

Isaiah 40:1–11; Psalm 96:1–2, 3, 10ac, 11–12, 13; Matthew 18:12–14

O sing to the Lord a new song;
  sing to the Lord, all the earth.
Sing to the Lord, bless his name;
  tell of his salvation from day to day.
Declare his glory among the nations,
  his marvelous works among all the peoples.

(Psalm 96:1–3)

The Lord comes to his people. That calls for singing. There is always reason to sing a new song to the Lord because there are always new blessings to acclaim him for.

The heavens, the earth, the sea, the plains, the trees of the forest are called to be joyful in the presence of the Lord because the Lord is coming to rule the earth and all its peoples. The glory and the power of the Lord call out for joyous expression. The Lord is coming to rule the world with justice and equity. That calls for singing.

This psalm is particularly suitable for Advent, as it celebrates the Lord's first coming. But it points forward equally well to the Second Coming: "The Lord our God comes with power."

Prayer

Angels of the heavenly choir, lead me into sacred song. Help me to surrender to a hymn of praise, and give me the voice to enter your song and the ears to recognize it. Amen.

Response

Plan to sing with your voice *and* heart the next time you come to Mass.

Wednesday of the Second Week of Advent

Isaiah 40:25–31; Psalm 103:1–2, 3–4, 8, 10; Matthew 11:28–30

Take my yoke upon you, and learn from me; for I am gentle and humble in heart, and you will find rest for your souls. For my yoke is easy, and my burden is light.

(Matthew 11:28–30)

These early Advent readings invite us to look forward to the coming of the Lord. They also tell us what kind of Lord we are looking for. It is a Lord of healing the sick and feeding multitudes. It is a Lord who offers security. It is a Lord who forgives sin.

Today's reading from Matthew 11 is a kind of summary. It tells us how Jesus sees himself. He is a giver of release and rest. He is kind and gentle, and makes things easy for those who respond to him. He is unwilling to weigh down the shoulders of those he loves.

That's the Jesus that offered himself to his earliest hearers. That's also the Jesus who offers himself to us today.

Prayer

Jesus, come to me and ease my burdens. Lift the weight of worry. Release me from all anxiety, so that I might rest in your arms without concern. Amen.

Response

Sit quietly in your favorite chair and ask Jesus to hold you for a few minutes.

Thursday of the Second Week of Advent

Isaiah 41:13–20; Psalm 145:1, 9, 10–11, 12–13; Matthew 11:11–15

When the poor and needy seek water,
  and there is none,
  and their tongue is parched with thirst,
I the Lord will answer them,
  I the God of Israel will not forsake them.

(Isaiah 41:17)

God speaks words of encouragement to his people: "Fear not. Insignificant as you are, I will help you. You shall rejoice in the Lord. I will not forsake you. I will grasp your right hand. You shall rejoice in me."

God promises his people strength and fruitfulness. It all arises from his infinite creative power. There is no need for the people to attract his attention by their excellence or strength or virtue. God cares for them just because he loves them, even if they are no better than creeping things.

God's creative power is active in our lives, too, here and now. We need to be reminded occasionally of our need and God's generosity lest we overlook God's gifts or take them for granted.

Prayer

Thank you, God, for not giving up on me. Your love is constant; I know I cannot earn it. Even when I fall you are right there to pick me up. Your help is my treasure. Amen.

Response

Send a note of encouragement to someone who is struggling.

Friday of the Second Week of Advent

Isaiah 48:17–19; Psalm 1:1–2, 3, 4, 6; Matthew 11:16–19

Happy are those
 who do not follow the advice of the wicked,
or take the path that sinners tread,
 or sit in the seat of scoffers;
but their delight is in the law of the Lord,
 and on his law they meditate day and night.
(Psalm 1:1–2)

The refrain for today's Responsorial Psalm is not from the book of Psalms but from the Gospel According to John. Jesus promises his followers light and life.

Light and life come to those who walk in the ways of the Lord. Following God's ways brings roots to our lives that can come from no source other than the law of the Lord and ongoing reflection and delight in his presence.

By contrast, the ways of the wicked yield only dry chaff, fruitless and unproductive.

This Responsorial Psalm and its refrain present us with a challenge. The quality of our lives are determined by the path that we follow. What path am I following in my life? What kind of harvest is it likely to produce?

Prayer

Light of the World, illuminate my earthly journey. Show me your way and protect me from the path of greed, evil, and sin. Give me sure vision to follow your path. Amen.

Response

In the dark of night, light a candle and reflect on the ways God's law is a light in your life.

Saturday of the Second Week of Advent

Sirach 48:1–4, 9–11; Psalm 80:2–3, 15–16, 18–19; Matthew 17:9a, 10–13

I tell you that Elijah has already come, and they did not recognize him, but they did to him whatever they pleased. So also the Son of Man is about to suffer at their hands.

(Matthew 17:12)

In the Gospel Reading for today, Jesus is speaking to his apostles about Elijah who was expected to return to prepare the way for the Messiah. In our Old Testament Reading, we hear the wise man Sirach giving an overview of Elijah's accomplishments.

God sends spokesmen to proclaim his message to his people: strong, brave, assertive men like Elijah and John the Baptist—and Jesus. They come at the time appointed for them and deliver the message that God has given to them.

We, too, are invited to be God's spokespeople. This doesn't mean calling down fire or bringing famine on the earth. Rather it's a vocation to give calm and constant witness to our dedication to the presence and word of the Lord.

Prayer

Emmanuel, give me the wisdom to be your presence in this world. Help me to speak up for your Gospel when necessary, to walk with the poor and oppressed, to listen to the brokenhearted, and to see you in the least among us. Amen.

Response

Do what you think Jesus would do in your interactions with everyone you meet today.

Third Sunday of Advent

Year A: *Isaiah 35:1–6a, 10; Psalm 146:6–7, 8–9, 9–10; James 5:7–10; Matthew 11:2–11*

Year B: *Isaiah 61:1–2a, 10–11; Luke 1:46–48, 49–50, 53–54; 1 Thessalonians 5:16–24; John 1:6–8, 19–28*

Year C: *Zephaniah 3:14–18a; Isaiah 12:2–3, 4, 5–6; Philippians 4:4–7; Luke 3:10–18*

Rejoice always, pray without ceasing, give thanks in all circumstances; for this is the will of God in Christ Jesus for you.

(1 Thessalonians 5:16–18)

This reading is a call to hope, and it constitutes the agenda for Christian believers of every age.

Our life as believers is not a list of dos and don'ts and rules to keep. Our life as believers is a matter of working with the Lord to bring his world to fulfillment, of doing our part to bring about ultimate happiness for all those who will accept it. And the Lord promises to work with us, just because he loves us, just because he is faithful.

Real Christian believers are people of hope. They know that they have wonderful things to look forward to in the ultimate future, but they also know that today and tomorrow are the context for God's blessings, too. That's why they "give thanks in all circumstances." That's why they "rejoice always."

Prayer

My soul rejoices in you, O God, and in your wondrous works. You fill my days with hope, my nights with the comfort of your mercy and love. Amen.

Response

Do something today that brings you joy, then share that joy with another person.

Monday of the Third Week of Advent

Readings used if today's date is
not December 17 or 18:
*Numbers 24:2–7, 15–17a; Psalm 25:4–5,
6–7, 8–9; Matthew 21:23–27*

The oracle of Balaam son of Beor,
   the oracle of the man whose eye is clear,
the oracle of one who hears the words of God,
   who sees the vision of the Almighty,
who falls down, but with eyes uncovered:
how fair are your tents, O Jacob,
   your encampments, O Israel!
                        (Numbers 24:3–5)

The Israelites were moving through the kingdom of Moab toward the Promised Land. Moab's king wanted to keep them out and called in Balaam, a sorcerer, to lay a curse on the Israelites.

In spite of his desire to do what the king wanted, Balaam couldn't. God compelled him to bless the Israelites. God was to make them prosper. They would be ruled by a king who would rise from the midst of the people like a star.

Christians have seen the Balaam narrative as a messianic prophecy. The new chosen people would prosper. A Messiah would rise like a star over his people. God's people still prosper. The Messiah shines over them like a star. Those who would do them harm find themselves powerless.

Prayer

You move your people to blessing, O Lord, and kindness shines down upon them like a star. Within this light we wait in joyful hope for the coming of your son, Jesus, and prepare in our hearts a home for him. Amen.

Response

Think of a time that you may have met someone who was prophetic and challenged the status quo. What did they say or do that made you consider your life in a different way?

Tuesday of the Third Week of Advent

Readings used if today's date is
not December 17 or 18:
Zephaniah 3:1–2, 9–13; Psalm 34:2–3, 6–7, 17–18, 19, 23; Matthew 21:28–32

This poor soul cried, and was heard by the Lord,
 and was saved from every trouble.
The angel of the Lord encamps
 around those who fear him, and delivers them.

(Psalm 34:6–7)

This is a song of confidence. In it we praise God, the defender of the poor.

God will hear the cry of the needy and will save them in time of distress. He is close to the poor and the brokenhearted. He pays special attention to them.

At some time or another we all find ourselves distressed, broken, poor, in need of God's help.

But whatever our trouble may be, we can be confident that the Lord will help us if we call on him. Our need for his attention constitutes our claim on him.

In Advent we look forward to the Lord's coming to care for us and enliven us and defend us and save us.

"The Lord hears the cry of the poor."

Prayer

Lord, console me in my weakness, raise me up to the heights of the angels where I may reflect your light and love. Amen.

Response

Find a way to give something to someone who is poorer than you, whether money, time, or some other form of help.

Wednesday of the Third Week of Advent

Readings used if today's date is not December 17 or 18:
Isaiah 45:6b–8, 18, 21b–25; Psalm 85: 9–10, 11–12, 13–14; Luke 7:18–23

John summoned two of his disciples and sent them to the Lord to ask, "Are you the one who is to come, or are we to wait for another?"

(Luke 7:18–19)

It's not clear whether John sent his disciples to Jesus in today's reading because he himself wanted to discover whether Jesus was the Messiah or because he wanted his disciples to experience the answer for themselves. In any case, the question is clear: Are you the one we're waiting for?

Jesus suggests that they figure things out for themselves. The blind see. The lame walk. The poor have the Gospel preached to them. In effect, Jesus says to the questioners, "You ought to be able to draw your own conclusions."

Who is Jesus for us? He forgives our sins. He feeds us with his Body and Blood. He strengthens our weaknesses. It shouldn't be hard to draw the right conclusion from data like that.

Prayer

Jesus, look into my heart and soul today, and heal the sins that I cling to so tightly. Create in me a clean heart, O Lord. Amen.

Response

Is there an area of your life that could use some revision? Think about one way you can better prepare to celebrate the birth of Jesus at Christmas.

Thursday of the Third Week of Advent

Readings used if today's date is not December 17 or 18:
Isaiah 54:1–10; Psalm 30:2, 4, 5–6, 11–12, 13; Luke 7:24–30

For a brief moment I abandoned you,
   but with great compassion I will gather you.
In overflowing wrath for a moment
   I hid my face from you,
but with everlasting love I will have compassion
      on you,
   says the Lord, your Redeemer.

(Isaiah 54:7–8)

The Lord coming to his people is a Lord of generosity and forgiveness.

He promises his people a multitude of offspring as a sign of his love for them. Their families will spread abroad to the right and left.

There may have been tension and struggle between God and his people, but the Lord now promises not to be angry any longer. Outbursts of God's wrath are now a thing of the past. God calls his people back and promises that his love will never again leave them.

During Advent, we prepare for the coming of the Lord. God calls us to be mindful of his generosity toward us and his forgiveness. He loves us in spite of our sins. He is a God of mercy.

Prayer

God of all creation, you have given me many gifts and many blessings. My heart overflows with gratitude for your abundant generosity. Teach me to give as you do, without bounds or reservation. Amen.

Response

Is there someone you are angry with, maybe have been for a long time? Resolve to start the process of releasing that anger, working toward forgiveness.

Friday of the Third Week of Advent

Readings used if today's date is
not December 17 or 18:
*Isaiah 56:1–3a, 6–8; Psalm 67:2–3,
5, 7–8; John 5:33–36*

Let the peoples praise you, O God;
  let all the peoples praise you.

The earth has yielded its increase;
  God, our God, has blessed us.

(Psalm 67:5, 6)

This is a song of corporate thanksgiving. It is not just an individual who is invited to offer thanks to God, but all the ends of the earth.

This psalm offers a statement of purpose for the whole cosmos, for all creation. It all exists so that God may be praised, so that his goodness may be acknowledged by all the nations of the earth.

When we praise God, we are most in touch with our final goal, most what God made us to be, most our best self. Likewise, when we lead others to praise God, we are keeping them in touch with their ultimate purpose.

Advent calls us all to reach out to the Lord. "O God, may all the nations praise you."

Prayer

God of all, your kingdom reaches throughout the world. Each person bears within them the spark of your abundant love, and mirrors your face. Let us grow each day in our love and respect for all your creatures and for all creation. Amen.

Response

Do something that helps you honor God's great cosmos. Take a walk; spend time meditating on a beautiful scene from nature; open your arms wide to breathe in the fresh, cool air of this bountiful earth.

December 17

*Genesis 49:2, 8–10; Psalm 72:3–4,
7–8, 17; Matthew 1:1–17*

So all the generations from Abraham to David are fourteen generations; and from David to the deportation to Babylon, fourteen generations; and from the deportation to Babylon to the Messiah, fourteen generations.

(Matthew 1:17)

Today we begin a series of Advent readings that prepare us more immediately for the Lord's birth. We start with the genealogy of Jesus as preserved by Matthew.

This family tree teaches us that Jesus came of a long line of all kinds of people: rich and poor, prominent and insignificant. Some are saints. Some are egregious sinners. But they are all human and Jesus is related to them all.

This reading invites us to take comfort in their—our—common humanity. Jesus has personal connections with all these people—and they are people like us. The Messiah who was to come is not an outsider. He is as human as we are. That's something to reflect on and be grateful for.

Prayer

O Wisdom from on high, reaching with power and might throughout all creation, come to your people and show us your salvation. Amen.

Response

Take a few minutes to reflect on some of the people in your family who most influenced you. What made them special? How do you mirror those qualities?

Fourth Sunday of Advent

Year A: *Isaiah 7:10–14; Psalm 24:1–2, 3–4, 5–6; Romans 1:1–7; Matthew 1:18–24*

Year B: *2 Samuel 7:1–5, 8b–12, 14a, 16; Psalm 89:2–3, 4–5, 27, 29; Romans 16:25–27; Luke 1:26–38*

Year C: *Micah 5:1–4a; Psalm 80:2–3, 15–16, 18–19; Hebrews 10:5–10; Luke 1:39–45*

Now to God who is able to strengthen you according to my gospel and the proclamation of Jesus Christ, according to the revelation of the mystery that was kept secret for long ages but is now disclosed….

(Romans 16:25–26)

Our life is not just an individual, private occurrence in the thousands of years of the world's history. Our life is part of the mystery of Christ. It's a carefully crafted episode in God's plan to extend the life and work of Jesus through all places and all times.

When God became a human being at that moment of the Annunciation to Mary, he gave a whole new dimension to the life of each one of us. We have a different significance than we would otherwise have had. Each of us is precious, each of us is important because we share the life of Christ, because we share Christ's mission to bring the world back to God.

Glory be to God, indeed.

Prayer

Blessed be the Lord, the God of Israel. You have raised up in our sight a savior, born to guide us in the way of peace. Amen.

Response

Where do you most see the mystery of God at work in your life?

December 18

Jeremiah 23:5–8; Psalm 72:1, 12–13, 18–19; Matthew 1:18–24

The days are surely coming, says the Lord, when I will raise up for David a righteous Branch, and he shall reign as king and deal wisely, and shall execute justice and righteousness in the land.

(Jeremiah 23:5)

Jeremiah was the prophet of doom par excellence. He was called to speak God's message to the Jews in the last years before the Babylonians overtook Jerusalem and destroyed it.

In this passage, however, Jeremiah is atypically positive. He looks forward to a time when God's people will be saved and dwell in security, when there will be a wise king who will govern with justice. The people will be more glorious than it was at the time of its liberation from Egypt.

God is showing Jeremiah the messianic future, a time of justice and prosperity. Christians have seen the fulfillment of this future in the coming of Jesus. He will bring the people to a new kind of security. He will be our justice.

Prayer

O Lord of Israel, who spoke to Moses in the burning bush and rescued your people from slavery, come, set us free! Amen.

Response

Are you ready to celebrate the birth of Jesus? Reflect on your efforts to prepare your heart during this Advent season, and see what is left to do.

December 19

Judges 13:2–7, 24–25; Psalm 71:3–4, 5–6, 16–17; Luke 1:5–25

For you, O Lord, are my hope,
  my trust, O Lord, from my youth.
Upon you I have leaned from my birth;
  it was you who took me from my mother's womb.
My praise is continually of you.

(Psalm 71:5–6)

The Lord is coming. He brings with him refuge and safety and hope and rescue.

Throughout our lives, from beginning to end, God is our help and our defense. He forgives our sins. He strengthens our weaknesses. He enlightens our darkness. He makes allowance for our limitations.

From before our birth he has been the source of confidence and strength for us. He is our stronghold, our fortress, our rock of refuge.

In return we owe him acknowledgment of his gifts to us. We owe him thanksgiving. We owe him praise, not just once in a while but always. Blessing the Lord should be our leitmotif, the basic theme of our existence.

"My mouth shall be filled with praise and I will sing your glory."

Prayer

O Flower of Jesse's stem, nations bow down before you; you have been raised up as a sign for your people. Come to our aid! Amen.

Response

How will you celebrate Christmas this year? Is there someone you know who may need an invitation to your celebration? Call them.

DECEMBER 20

Isaiah 7:10–14; Psalm 24:1–2, 3–4, 5–6; Luke 1:26–38

Again the Lord spoke to Ahaz, saying "Ask a sign of the Lord your God; let it be deep as Sheol or high as heaven." But Ahaz said, "I will not ask, and I will not put the Lord to the test."

(Isaiah 7:10–12)

This reading is messianic par excellence.

King Ahaz has entered an alliance with the Assyrians. Isaiah has warned the king to rely on the Lord and he wouldn't need the Assyrians' help. God offers to give Ahaz a sign of his care for his people. Ahaz effectively responds, "Let's keep God out of this. I can handle things myself." Isaiah says that God will give the king a sign anyway. "A virgin shall conceive and bear a son and shall name him Emmanuel," meaning, "God with us."

We don't know to whom Isaiah was referring, but Christian believers have always interpreted the prophecy as referring to the virgin Mary giving birth to Jesus, the Messiah.

God was with his people then. He still is now.

Prayer

O Key of David, you who break down the prison walls of death for all who dwell in darkness and sin, free us from captivity. Amen.

Response

Say three Hail Marys today, then spend a few minutes reflecting on what Mary means to your faith life.

DECEMBER 21

Song of Songs 2:8–14 or Zephaniah 3:14–18;
Psalm 33:2–3, 11–12, 20–21; Luke 1:39–45

Elizabeth was filled with the Holy Spirit and exclaimed with a loud cry, "Blessed are you among women, and blessed is the fruit of your womb. And why has this happened to me, that the mother of my Lord comes to me?"

(Luke 1:41–43)

Today's Gospel recounts the meeting of Mary and Elizabeth. It's a wonderful passage, full of life, abundance, and wisdom. The words of the story nearly jump off the page.

Both women have been touched by God's providence. Each is joyful over what God has done for her and for the other. Each recognizes the saving power of God at work. Each is inspired to a lyrical outburst of praise. We hear Elizabeth's song of happiness today. In tomorrow's Gospel Reading we will hear Mary's.

Most of us don't break out in poetry when something good happens to us. But that doesn't mean that there's no reason to be joyful. God is always working his loving plans out in all of us. There's always reason for gratitude.

Prayer

O Radiant Dawn, fount of eternal light, shine on those who live in darkness and in the shadow of death. Amen.

Response

As you go about your day, hold the image of Jesus inside you and imagine that, like Mary, you carry him before the time of his birth.

December 22

1 Samuel 1:24–28; 2:1, 4–5, 6–7, 8abcd; Luke 1:46–56

Hannah prayed and said, "My heart exults in the Lord; my strength is exalted in my God. My mouth derides my enemies, because I rejoice in my victory."

(1 Samuel 2:1)

Today's Responsorial Psalm is a hymn attributed to Hannah, mother of Samuel, last of the judges of Israel.

Hannah gives thanks to God because she has borne a son despite her previous sterility. She praises God as helper of the weak who alone is the source of true strength. The Lord is the giver of life who makes the poor rich, who raises up the lowly, who makes the needy glorious.

This canticle has many points of resemblance to Mary's Magnificat, the song of praise that Mary sang when she visited her cousin Elizabeth.

As we approach the celebration of Jesus's birth, the Church invites us to give thanks for God's intervention in the affairs of humanity, to take joy in the Lord.

Prayer

O King of all nations, joy of every human heart, come and save the creature you fashioned from dust. Amen.

Response

Take some time to help someone who may be stressed or anxious today.

December 23

Malachi 3:1–4, 23–24; Psalm 25:4–5, 8–9, 10, 14; Luke 1:57–66

See, I am sending my messenger to prepare the way before me, and the Lord whom you seek will suddenly come to his temple. The messenger of the covenant in whom you delight—indeed, he is coming, says the Lord of hosts.

(Malachi 3:1)

The book of Malachi is the last book of the Old Testament. It leads its readers out of the preliminary revelation into the world of redemption by Christ.

Today the prophet looks forward to the advent of the Lord who will come to purify his people, to bring a new era of holiness. But before the coming of the Lord there will be an initial stage. Elijah the prophet will return to prepare the people to receive the Lord.

In what Malachi promises, it is easy to see the coming of Jesus, the Messiah, preceded by John the Baptist, the forerunner, who would renew the people for their new relationship with God.

God had elaborate plans for salvation. Those plans are still being fulfilled today.

Prayer

O come, Emmanuel, desire of the nations and savior of all people. Come, set us free! Amen.

Response

What last-minute tasks are left for you to do before Christmas? Take the time to do each with love.

December 24

2 Samuel 7:1–5, 8–11, 16; Psalm 89:2–3, 4–5, 27, 29; Luke 1:67–79

By the tender mercy of our God,
  the dawn from on high will break upon us,
to give light to those who sit in darkness and in
  the shadow of death,
to guide our feet into the way of peace.
(Luke 1:78–79)

We come to the end of these cameo appearances of Joseph and Mary and Elizabeth and Zechariah with the Canticle of Zechariah.

This is a song of salvation that the Church repeats each day at morning prayer. First it tells of all that God has done in the past to save and strengthen and enlighten and reassure his people. Then it tells of what God will continue to do for us through the mission of Zechariah's son, John. Through John God will continue to care for us and lead us on the way to peace.

God wants to come to us and be with us and share his life with us. That's what salvation means. That's what Advent and Christmas are all about.

Prayer

O God, on this day before we celebrate the birth of your son, bring peace and joy to those who suffer, healing to those who are ill, comfort to those who mourn, and food to the hungry. May all your people feel your tender love and mercy today. Amen.

Response

Light a candle or put on a light that is not needed, and keep it lit throughout the day as a reminder of the Light of the World.

Christmas Day

Isaiah 52:7–10; Psalm 98:1, 2–3, 3–4, 5–6;
Hebrews 1:1–6; John 1:1–18

Long ago God spoke to our ancestors in many and various ways by the prophets, but in these last days he has spoken to us by a Son, whom he appointed heir of all things, through whom he also created the worlds.

(Hebrews 1:1–2)

When our text says that, in these last days, God "has spoken to us by a Son," it means that the finality of revelation that we have in the Son consists in the reality of God that is offered for us to share through the humanness of Christ. There is no more to be revealed because we have been offered the very fullness of God.

Living in Christ is not one way of salvation among many others. It is the one, unique access to himself that God the Father has given to us. The fact remains that salvation comes only through Christ and that Christ comes only through the gift of the Father.

That gift is what we celebrate on Christmas. *Gloria in excelsis Deo!*

PRAYER

Glory to God in the highest, and on earth peace to people of goodwill.

RESPONSE

Be thankful for all God has given you, especially the gift of his Son, Jesus.